Sometimes You Gotta Lose the Mansion

Susan Underhill

The Story Behind the Story

In 2011, after +25 years of working for corporate America... Susan developed a business plan, researched the market and landscape, leveraged her 401K/Pension, quit her job, packed up her belongings and traveled +900 miles to open a vacation retreat. Susan purchased a historic Mansion in downtown Denver, and after several intense months of renovations, repairs and retrofitting the Mansion which for years had been used as a law office, officially unlocked the gates in December, and greeted her first arrivals.

This is her story of triumphs, trials, and tribulations of opening and operating a small business. She shares her mixed story with the simplicity and sophistication in keeping with her approach to how she operated the Emerson Mansion. Every chapter captures and tells a true and inspiring moment and how she personally overcame many of the common pitfalls of being an entrepreneur. It is meant to be a quick, concise read that will allow the reader to engage and rewrite each chapter on how or what they would do differently.

Nestled in a thriving urban Denver neighborhood, just blocks from downtown, the Emerson Mansion provided the setting of the story and hosted +450 guests from over 20 countries each with an endearing story.

Along the way so many people contributed to her story. Although, this is Susan's journey; the complexity of the words and magic of the illustrations could not have been done without the collaboration of Cindy and Dawn, who were from the very beginning a part of her journey. All three took on this writing project with vengeance and it is their first published work together as well as alone. It is a testimony on no matter the scope of the project; heed her advice to never go it alone, as the journey is always better shared.

Sometimes You Gotta Lose the Mansion

By

Susan Underhill

1st Printing – 2014

Table of Contents

One
Going from stuck to unstuck

A quick browse through the business/marketing section of your local bookstore or a comparable search with omnipresent online book retailer Amazon.com and you're likely to find seemingly hundreds of "what I did that was brilliant and how you can do it, too" stories. Sure, there's value in those and I've read my share. Fewer and further between, however, is the rare someone who says "here's what I did wrong and here's how YOU can learn from it." Not that my business was one of complete failure; quite the contrary. I had some great successes and, don't worry, we'll review those as well. But the value in sharing this experience is to help others benefit by becoming more aware of common entrepreneurial and new business pitfalls. My story is somewhat unique though the missteps along the way are ones that many have made before me and many more will make in the future. If I can lay a road map that helps even a few people navigate around these common mistakes while encouraging the nascent business owner/entrepreneur to reach for their dreams and never look back, then the value of this experience compounds exponentially for me.

Where are you right now? Perhaps you're in specialty boutique shop, a novelty store, a funky clothes store, or a florist? Were you browsing and stumbled upon this book and thought, "that's odd... what's this doing here?" The placement of this book is by specific design to, from start to finish, capture an experience for you. I want the process of reading this book to be unique. I want you to remember where and when you bought this book because it was out of the ordinary. Throughout the book I hope to push you, engage you, bend your comfort zone and encourage you to think about your dreams (and your fears) in a unique and different way. I want you to use this book to explore your potential to succeed AND to fail. Yes, you read that right – explore your potential to fail. Get this, if you think you can't or won't fail then you won't be ready to do something about it when you see your hard work heading south. And, I believe, that somewhere between your greatest professional high and your potential (or realized) ultimate low there is a sweet spot where you can thrive. But how can you find that place if you don't know the outer reaches?

Though I didn't know it at the time, I left my corporate career to pursue the full spectrum of my ability. In many ways, the corporate life was very easy; it was comfortable, stable, and low risk. However, throughout my career in Corporate America I always found myself struggling to be the "good employee," kind of like the good wife in a very bad marriage. Like most bad marriages, it left me feeling very unfulfilled. Tenacity being my strong-suit, my career in Corporate America was fueled by my love for tackling a problem and wrestling it to the ground. Eventually, the reward of wrangling challenges couldn't keep my frustrations at bay. Gallup's definition of an entrepreneur is a person who finds solutions to problems (Gallup). I was a solution-oriented person trapped in a problem that I couldn't seem to solve. In my "lifetime" as a corporate employee I had my share of good, bad and ugly management styles but none as ugly as my last manager. He thrived on his covert ability in tormenting and bullying his subordinates into compliance. When it came to creativity, execution, and understanding metrics; he was stupid. My ultimate "a-ha" moment was the day I realized, I just can't fix stupid. That was where I was stuck.

Do you know why manhole covers are round? This is a question that often appears on intelligence tests and entrance exams for many elite universities and companies. The answer: A round cover can't fall into the manhole, no matter how much you twist and turn it. A rectangular cover can, all you have to do is twist sideways. Just like that round manhole covers, I was never going to fit into their square box. When I finally embraced that idea I became free to look the only two obvious choices square in the face: I could stay in a mode of constant combat with the infrastructure of corporate hierarchy or I could pursue my dream of being my own boss. In an attempt to get myself and my career unstuck, I took the leap. Unfortunately, I didn't heed the signs that this change was imminent as my office and house had become cluttered with magnets, postcards, books, and framed pictures depicting quotes and inspirational messages about empowerment and change. So, instead of making a strategic exit, I left in crisis. A self created crisis that led to an intense period of growth, discovery, and learning about the outer reaches of my professional spectrum.

So What?

Although, the final destination of my first solo flight, and the accuracy of my navigation are still to be determined, my life is richer, and more complete than ever before. Simon Sinek, author of *Start With Why*, was very influential in helping me take the leap from Corporate America. Reading Sinek's book, *Start With Why*, helped to decode and demystify what I could not verbalize and was therefore, according to his theory, too scared to do. However for passion to survive, it needs structure. A why without the how, has a very high probability of failure.

Achieving success has two parts: Defining your dream and putting together a plan of attack to go after it. By the time I left my corporate job, I knew my dream was to run a retreat venue targeting professional women who wanted to reconnect with their most healthy self. Interestingly, I had become my own target audience. By staying too long in a job I despised, I was left too depleted emotionally and intellectually to realize the shortcomings in my execution plan. In my corporate job, did I gain expertise, maturity, and a small nest egg? Absolutely and I couldn't' have done it without the benefits of this experience! But I lost sight of myself in the process; I became angry and within that emotion created an unnecessary crisis for myself.

Would I make the leap again? **Abso-fucking-lutely.** I am stronger, smarter, happier, more humble, and more grateful today than ever!

Now What?

Think of this book as a mixed drink: A shaker full of candid, real-life business experience mixed with shot of inspiration, a few shots of entertainment, and a just a hint of bitters and sweet. The end result is intended to be intoxicating, invigorating, and immensely informative. When you find yourself at the last page, my hope is that this book has been fully consumed – tattered and torn, pages bent and earmarked, each section sprinkled with notes in sharpie pen, pencil, highlighter, crayon or whatever you had handy when you just HAD to write down that creative thought or brilliant idea. Business ownership demands creativity. Creativity thrives in spontaneity. By learning to be mentally nimble and creative under pressure you will be better prepared to tackle the many challenges that may come your way while you reach to achieve your dreams.

Let's follow these steps to start to outline your roadmap for realizing the full spectrum of your potential:

- ✓ Allow yourself to dream - A LOT. Then start to work on your plan.
- ✓ When planning, play the devil's advocate. Ask "why"

at every step through the process.

✓ Spin your dream into a product or service that will be used every single day.

✓ If you don't love it, why should anyone buy it?

✓ What problem will your dream solve?

✓ Do you know everything about your competitors? Learn it and learn from their experiences.

✓ What does the launch of your business look like?

✓ How will you garner a predictable revenue stream?

✓ Are you ready to quit your day job?!

✓ Take baby steps before you take your leaps.

✓ Don't go it alone, at least not for very long.

✓ Never look back.

WhtWldSusanSay@twitter.com

"Write your own story, sing your own song, and dance your own dance; just get your ass moving ... and never, ever let a pussy torment, bully or determine your destiny."

What Would You Say?

_____

_____

_____

_____

_____

_____

_____

_____

_____

_____

_____

_____

_____

_____

_____

_____

_____

_____

Two.
What's in your toolbox?
(How to start smart as you launch your business.)

←——————◉——————→

Nothing good ever seems to come from actions inspired by 3 AM panic attacks. The one that happened the first night I slept in the mansion I had purchased to operate my urban retreat center was no exception. Possibly, my first tip-off that I was going off course might have been that I was alone in a mansion, ripping up carpet in my underwear at o'dark-thirty. At that point, if the neighbors have peered in the windows they would have been justified in thinking, "Oh, I see, they just sold the mansion to be used as an insane asylum."

Actually, maybe one of the neighbors did witness that episode... it might start to explain some of their later actions. Regardless, the fact remains, there I was, the owner of a mansion, covered in remnants of carpet padding in my skivvies in the middle of night and a brilliant question occurred to me; "what in the hell am I doing?!" I must have thought that was a rhetorical question because I certainly didn't stop with my middle-of-the-night remodeling project to analyze my actions. Not only did I keep on with the carpet but in the following months I immersed myself in the fine arts of plumbing, interior decorating, wallpaper removal, electrical engineering, turn-of-the-century radiator maintenance (with no manuals), and management of five different fuse boxes randomly scattered throughout the building. Let me say, for the record, as you start your business realize this is an adventure that no MBA will prepare you for. You'd be better off taking some vocational education classes at a local community college. Or better yet consider finding a plumber to date.

So What?

When starting this business, I wasn't looking to diversify my skill set. I didn't take on this project hoping to refine my remodeling skills, to build my portfolio, so that I could later land a bigger, better remodeling gig. When put like that it sounds ridiculous, doesn't it?

By this point, you might be thinking why in the hell did she purchase a historic mansion with those inherent problems in lieu of perhaps leasing? Believe me, there was a lot of thought and due diligence put into other options, but leasing would have required even more build-outs without any ownership should I go out of business down the road. The mistake was not in the fact that I purchased the Mansion, but more in how I didn't establish a "go-to market" strategy complete with timelines and execution plans. All these are things which I had done thousands of times in my old role and could practically do in my sleep. It's almost ironic how I forgot to apply so much of what I had learned and executed successfully over the years. In my corporate job I was required to vet my ideas with senior leadership but because I was without a board of seasoned executives or an operating committee to submit ideas, plans and seek advice, I didn't have anyone to push back and show me the holes in my ideas. I had taken the value of this protocol for granted. One of the great things about being an entrepreneur is that you don't need approval of your ideas, but I would suggest going it alone is not completely healthy either.

The ultimate desire of most entrepreneurs in pursuit of their big visions and dreams is to not have to obtain approval and consensus on decisions. Though, oftentimes that is the very thing that we need. Our heart and head gets caught in the dust and confusion of the construction debris and we don't see flaws in our most well thought-out plans.

My suggestion is to install either a formal or informal advisory committee or board that you can bounce ideas off of, get solid feedback even when you don't want to hear it, and to provide you with great business-to-business networking. Diversify your board members to compliment your skill set. Think of it as Skill Gap Insurance. If possible, pay them a fee or give them in-kind contributions or trade services, but always, always recognize them. Professionals love to be recognized and often times will provide help and guidance for the mere recognition. Pick your board members with care, seek their advice, trust and reward them. Be creative in developing the rewards, find their Achilles' heel.

Being trained in the corporate world does have its advantages. The training and skills acquired are incredibly valuable, no matter what your aspirations are. My situation is no exception. The corporate world had prepared me well, but I forgot to unpack my corporate toolbox, and re-engineer these tools to build my new venture.

Strength Finder is a great program developed by Marcus Buckingham & Donald Clifton while working for Gallup. (Clifton M. B., 2001) It was extremely helpful for me in determining my dominant characteristics and leadership style. I would highly recommend purchasing *Strength Finder 2.0* and taking the online assessments (Rath, 2007). It allowed me to tap into my natural talents, which has been validated by the many years working with my corporate counterparts. Based on my Strength Finder assessment my natural strengths are: Command, Strategic, Achiever, Individualization, and Activator.

Here's an explanation of my known Achilles' heels and how that knowledge translates into the traits I should have sought out in the people to be on my Advisory Board:

✓ I seek out situations with inherent resistance, this can be intimidating to people and my reaction can be dismissive - Choose a diplomat.
✓ I need enough information but get impatient with information overload - Choose someone who is data-oriented and will slow the bus down if necessary.
✓ I am a natural delegator – Choose someone who can help provide oversight.
✓ I notice and appreciate details and customization –

Choose someone who will help point out cost/benefit analysis of these upgrades.

✓ I challenge people more than I should – Choose someone who can assist in being selective with phrases or has experience with PR or HR skills.

✓ I like to make things happen and can be impatient with people who are slow and need more time - Choose "action" oriented people to be on your team.

Once you learn your strengths, cater to them. Acquire and/or surround yourself with talent that will compliment or fill a void. Always keep in mind that you can outsource many talents. Hiring and managing full or part time in-house employees can be exhausting. Outsourcing can give you a competitive edge, allow you to hire expertise you can't afford initially, and give you access to some of the best and brightest, as increasingly these days, many prefer to work as independent contractors. Don't view this strictly as an expense; realize that it is an investment, one you cannot afford NOT to make.

Now What?

✓ Create your own Advisory Board.

✓ Determine your personality profiles by taking proven assessments.

✓ Which skill gaps do you have?

✓ Determine what types of professionals will compliment your skills sets?

✓ How often will you meet with them?

✓ Collectively or Individually?

✓ How will you compensate or recognize their contributions?

WhtWldSusanSay@twitter.com

"Starting your own business is tough. Get manicures, pedicures, change your lipstick color every season, keep your hair in style and buy a really cool helmet."

→ What Would You Say?

_____

_____

_____

_____

_____

_____

_____

_____

_____

_____

_____

_____

_____

_____

_____

_____

_____

_____

Three
Your one thing
(It's a saturated marketplace;
learn to stand out in the crowd)

If you've done much networking you are familiar with the "30 second commercial." All networking events seem to commence with forcing their constituents to perform some annoyingly snappy and condensed version of the essence of their business, the infamous elevator speech.

When I first started networking in Denver my "pitch" involved a diatribe about my business, Fit, Fueled & Focused, and how I was passionate about providing professional women a retreat environment where they could rejuvenate through physical fitness, healthy food, and a reconnection to any part of their mind, body or spirit lost in the daily shuffle of life. I'd go on to explain how my program was customized to the working executive, encompassing either a short-version weekend junket or a more extensive week-long program. I discussed how all the market research indicated vacations were trending toward focusing on fitness and healthy life habits. Ok... I'll admit, I wasn't so good at the 30 second thing, see I prefer taking the stairs over an elevator any day of the week.

After a solid month of watching eyes glaze over while I explained my business, one night at an "after hours" networking event (read: libations were involved and I had partaken) when asked that fateful question, "What do you do?" I replied demurely, "I own a big fucking mansion!" which provoked an instant roar of laughter (and a few gasps). My previously uninterested listener suddenly became VERY intrigued. Several times through the conversation she pulled other colleagues into the conversation, introducing me by way of, "This is Susan and she owns a mansion!"

That abrupt response came from a place of frustration and desperation but the surprising reaction was a lesson that I will never forget. When I refined my pitch to one that was unique for the business networking environment, I became more interesting and memorable. In fact, at future events when I introduced myself, people would respond, "I heard about you and the Manson, I want to know more." Really, I went from a 30 second elevator speech to a 10 second express ride, and it only took a four letter word, ooops, I mean four words: "I own a Mansion."

So What?

From that moment on, inquiries about my venue (and about me) came fast and furious. Networking became fun (I can't believe I just said that). But, here's the thing - you don't have to own a mansion to be memorable. Everybody is unique and by virtue of that fact, what you bring to your business is unlike anyone else. Finding that differentiator is key to marketing your business. Sometimes though, like in my case, picking your strongest selling point requires some emotional detachment. Believe it or not, I was not that excited about owning a mansion. My dream was to own a hacienda; a mansion sounded stuffy and austere. Because of my personal feelings about the mansion, I chose to focus on my Fit, Fueled & Focused business model when I explained myself at networking events. Recognizing that this did not resonate with my audience (at least in that setting) took a big dose of checking my emotions and facing reality. Like it or not, when I started to embrace owning a mansion and created my networking pitch around that ONE fact, my business started to change.

Often business success is less about what you think you know and more about what you know your customers want or need. Owning a business requires you to be nimble, to change, and to be unemotional when the business requires it. Embracing this aspect of business ownership at the onset will ease some of the stress that comes with a start-up.

Now What?

Follow the process below to find your one thing:

- ✓ Start by describing your business in 20 words or less.
- ✓ Now circle the two - four words in that 20 that most represent the essence of your business.
- ✓ Open up a search window on your computer and enter those 2 - 4 terms (include your city or town if the business is primarily marketed locally)
- ✓ Look at what is displayed in the top 10 search results.

✓ Go to each website and look at the home page,

✓ How are you different? How do you want to be different? How can you set yourself apart from the others?

✓ Don't forget to check your emotional attachment and take a critical eye to where the holes are in the marketplace and how your unique abilities can fill that void.

✓ Look around you. Find inspiration in personal possessions and things that represent who you are and what you are about that you can weave into your "one thing" to make it unique.

✓ Pick your marketplace differentiator using a healthy mix of creativity and emotional detachment.

WhtWldSusanSay@twitter.com

"Survival is all about how you handle Plan B"

→ What Would You Say?

_____

_____

_____

_____

_____

_____

_____

_____

_____

_____

_____

_____

_____

_____

_____

_____

_____

_____

_____

Four

Stay outta the weeds

(To grow your business you have to get out of your own way)

Interestingly, opening myself up to make the shift in how I associated with the Mansion ultimately caused a shift in how I would use the Mansion to generate revenue. In the process of trying to make ends meet, I decided to temporarily pause my retreat business ambitions and turn the Mansion into a Bed & Breakfast. Through this transition I had become a combination of everything I never wanted to be: handyman, subcontractor, painter, short-order cook, laundry/maid service, bed-maker, toilet cleaner, window washer, plumber, locksmith, night security patrol, day and night front desk attendant, tourist guide and booking agent. Yet it took a dramatic tumble down a flight of stairs and eminent threat of physical impairment before I realized what I was doing untenable.

The Mansion was four floors with no elevators. For the last 70 years it had been used for business offices, it had not been a residence since 1940. To say that it had not been modernized is an understatement. The Mansion was definitely not designed to accommodate the operations that are fundamental to running a bed & breakfast. For instance, due to plumbing and electrical capacities (combined with the fact that it was the fastest way to get them installed) the washer and dryer were located on different floors. How convenient, right? So, in addition to all the other odd jobs I was managing on a daily basis, countless was the number of times I scaled the many stairs between floors each day. Come to think of it, I should have worn a pedometer to record the distance traveled daily just within the walls of the Mansion. I was working non-stop, sleeping only in spurts as my guests' comings and goings allowed it. I was physically and emotionally tapped. Adrenaline was all that was keeping me going.

Late one night (or early one morning, actually), as I was scrambling to finish several loads of laundry, I descended the basement steps carrying not one but two heavy baskets of freshly washed towels to be dried. I tripped and tumbled down the two flights of stairs, landing prone on the basement floor unable to move. As I lay there, slowly taking inventory of my body parts and what damage had been done by the fall, for the first time in my life, I understood the meaning of terrified. One thought looped through my brain as I lay there: If I was to become physically disabled, either temporarily or permanently, all my hard work would be lost. Things had to change. And, sadly, it took a crisis of epic proportions for me to ask for help.

The next morning, very bruised both physically and psychologically, I found myself in my accountant's office looking for business advice. After just a couple short months of being a mansion proprietor I had every appearance of being, as the cowboys say; rode hard and put away wet. Since I hadn't put an advisory board into place (if you skipped chapter 3, now might be a good time to go back and read it) I was looking to any available professional willing to offer an opinion on how and when this torture was going to let up. When was I going to be allowed the time to be the creative entrepreneur I had dreamed of being? Showing an alarming lack of empathy for my plight, my accountant leaned back in his chair, chuckled and said, "You've become the pie lady!" You might be able to guess my response but to sum it up in my best texting shorthand --- WTF?!

He then reached in his desk and pulled out a book that would forever change the way I run a business. Over the next few days, I consumed *The E-Myth Revisited* a minimum of five times. I learned about the pie lady, I learned about the dueling personalities present within all entrepreneurs, I learned about "Entrepreneurial Seizure" and how of the four phases: exhilaration, terror, exhaustion and despair (Gerber, 1995), I was in phase three with only despair to look forward to if I didn't make a quick change.

So What?

After the fifth read of the book, I felt ready to embark on the task at hand; writing an operations manual for the Emerson Mansion. I felt absolutely confident that by putting a system into place, as if I were going to franchise my business model, and by streamlining every aspect of my business I could focus on running my business rather than allowing it to RUN me!

I do believe that the universe presents to you what you

need, when you need it. Without a doubt, that book was exactly what I needed to read in that moment. Relief doesn't start to describe how I felt to learn that the chemical make-up of an entrepreneur lends itself to multiple personalities who inherently don't like each other. My big vision entrepreneurial self had gotten trapped in the role of "technician" and, man, was I exhausted. Understanding the dynamics between these dueling personalities and a way to focus my energy so that I could get back to doing what I love, building my business not running a mansion. See, there is an important distinction there... for personality types like mine, I was passionate about developing and implementing a business, I was less passionate about owning and running a mansion. Though, truth be told, I did eventually come into my own with it and learned to enjoy certain nuances. Now, at times, I actually miss it. However, I welcomed the notion of removing myself from the day-to-day operations of the business. To do this successfully you must create (and use!) an operations manual for every single thing you do. Particularly when hiring, training, and incentivizing employees. And if you're thinking (like I did) that you cannot afford to hire employees - my guess is that when you factor it all out, you cannot afford NOT to hire employees. The trick is in not hiring expensive talent. You're the "talent." (Gerber, 1995) Look for employees who flourish in following standards, policies, and procedures. You want your employees to excel in delivering to your customers with zeal and consistency.

After reading some pretty impressive statistics and actually applying the principles to my business, I can honestly say that the franchise model is successful because it works and how it works can be easily applied to any business. Once you have defined the standard for your business then you can create systems and repeatable processes that any employee can execute which facilitates your ability to deliver on customer expectations.

Did you feel your hair stand up on end when you read that your business "can be run by anyone" or did you breathe a sigh of relief? Most people probably feel a rush of anxiety upon reading that because the idea of removing yourself from the business can be truly frightening.

Now What?

You don't need to be a franchise to be successful; just incorporate the franchise business model and you can harness the power that breeds success. Here are my suggestions for establishing an operations or procedures manual.

Definition of Your Services, Brand & Standards

- ✓ Create a statement, define standards, and establish colors & a logo that embrace the standard.
- ✓ Base your product on pricing points.
- ✓ What are your clients/markets willing to pay?

✓ Can you deliver your brand within these pricing points?

✓ Eliminate services that don't reflect your brand or the customer isn't willing to pay the price or see a value, no matter how important you think it is!

Organizational Strategy -
Create an well defined organization chart

✓ Develop Specific Titles & Job Descriptions

✓ Clarify Reporting Structure

✓ If you are performing those roles - Put your name within the Box and give yourself the title.

✓ If your name is in more than 2 or 3 boxes perhaps it is time to hire or outsource the function.

✓ If the function/job is vital to the delivery of the product you cannot delete it from the organizational chart.

Operations Strategy -
Develop specific check lists for every function/operation. Here is a small condensed excerpt from the Emerson Mansion Operations Manual.

✓ Dusting & Mopping the Main Area (30 Minutes)

✓ Bathrooms & Reading Room

(Inspected 3 Times Daily)

✓ Bedroom Turn Over (Time Required 20-30 Minutes)

✓ Food Inventory & Shopping List

✓ Breakfast Set Up & Procedures (1 Hour)

✓ Cocktail Set Up (1 Hour)

✓ Check In Procedures (15 Minutes)

✓ Check Out Procedures

(Prepared with Departing Gift)

✓ Bike Rental Procedures

People Strategy - How to Recognize, Reward & Motivate

✓ Abolishing of all performance reviews – Replace with Daily feed-back & role modeling. Performance reviews are only in place for inept managers to CYA (Cover their Asses). Besides if you do a superb job in defining your processes, expectations and boundaries, employees will self eliminate or voluntarily leave.

Find all of the numerous ways to say "Thank you" to your employees, and vendors every day!

✓ Thank you for being here.
✓ Thank you for smiling at the customer.

✓ Thank you for showing up on time.

✓ Thank you for dressing appropriately.

✓ Thank you for following the rules.

✓ Thank you for your energy.

WhtWldSusanSay@twitter.com

"All thanks you's have an expiration date, they need to be renewed every 24 hours."

What Would You Say?

_____

_____

_____

_____

_____

_____

_____

_____

_____

_____

_____

_____

_____

_____

_____

_____

_____

_____

_____

_____

_____

Five
Customers don't know jack

It was month 1 of the mansion being fully operational. Everything seemed to be in place; window coverings installed, smoke and carbon monoxide detectors functioning, linens fluffed, check-in and check-out procedures dialed in, and front door coded keyless entry installed. Even details that I feared would be a deterrent for guests, like shared bathrooms, were becoming less of an issue particularly since pinpointing the sector of my target market where price and other amenities trumped privacy. Though there was still one major detail that needed to be sorted out. Surprisingly, the term Bed & Breakfast asserts that with the accommodations guests will receive breakfast. While in my "soft launch" phase, I took surveys, asked for comments, read blogs, and directly queried my guests about their preferences for breakfast. I took every comment, suggestion and request to heart and when I finally found myself with a "full house" I decided to incorporate all of the well-intended suggestions and offer a full breakfast spread on the first morning. We're talking Easter Sunday brunch buffet caliber. I cooked buttermilk pancakes, served oozing with real butter and the best maple syrup, organic and cage free scrambled eggs, smoked antibiotic sausages, non-cured bacon, fried potatoes with scallions & jalapeños served with warm tortillas that could be softly folded into a scrumptious breakfast burritos, freshly squeezed orange and grapefruit juice, French pressed coffee paired with real cream and chocolate shavings, an assortment of teas, cereals, Greek yogurt, bagels all served alongside milk, fresh berries, real butter and cream cheeses. My spread was impressive; the coordination of preparing the items was mind-blowing and I painstakingly displayed the items meticulously. I had literally been up since 4 A.M. getting things ready; not just the food, but the dining room... fresh flowers in the vases, music playing softly, flatware, glass plates and stemware. My dining room looked AFA (absolutely fucking amazing). Exhausted, extremely proud and very excited to the see the warm faces of gratitude from my guests as they emerged from their rooms, I waited with anticipation.

Guess what? Regardless of what they thought they wanted, my guests didn't want breakfast. But they were in denial about it. They liked the IDEA that they would get breakfast with their stay but when presented with an amazing breakfast their response was, "thanks but no thanks." Don't get me wrong, they appreciated the effort. They just had other things in mind like sitting on the porch and enjoying a cup of coffee or reading the newspaper which, by the way, was the ONE thing I had forgotten! Seriously, not one person ate the hot breakfast. Not one. Two people thought about it but then opted for yogurt and berries. So, after my last guests departed for their day, I sat down with a cup of coffee and had a good ol' fashioned cry. Not just because my guests did not eat but because of the incredible waste that lay before me. As a start up, I simply could not afford to let things go to waste; not materials, not resources and particularly not my time. So, over the following week, I ate breakfast for breakfast, breakfast for lunch and breakfast for dinner. But what was done, was done. After the kitchen was cleaned and put away, my tears were dried, all that was left for me to do was pull up my big girl panties (which were expanding by the second!) hop on my bike and ride. You can bet your ass that I returned from my ride with a clearer head and a newfound set of priorities.

So What?

Bigger, better, faster, stronger, cheaper .... Bullshit. Why? If you're not strategically aligning your objectives and your output to your audience then your efforts are a colossal waste of resources. If your customers expect bigger, better, faster, stronger and you have established that expectation with a plan to follow-through then, by all means, go nuts. My point is, take the time to know more than your customers demographic and psychographic profiles. You've (presumably) spent all this effort carving out a business that is tailored to a specific target audience, use that knowledge to show your customers that you don't just know who they are and what they do but that you understand them, intimately. For example, all my instincts told me that what my guests wanted was a paper and coffee in the morning and a glass of wine or a beer in the evening. It was that simple. The Emerson Mansion was a unique B & B with its downtown location which attracted a certain type of clientele. I was getting three types of guests; business travelers, foreign travelers either on holiday or attending conferences (who were quite comfortable with the shared bathroom situation), and visiting parents of newly graduated, young professionals (particularly daughters) who had moved to downtown Denver and their parents were looking for inexpensive accommodations. The business guests were off early in the morning to meetings, the foreign travelers were enjoying the tastes and sights of Denver, and the parents were treating their young, broke kids to a decent breakfast. None of them were lingering around to dine with me. I wasn't listening to my intuition, and watching my guests' habits; I was listening and heeding what they were telling me they wanted. I knew what they wanted all along. They didn't.

Now what?

Customers will give you a lot of feedback but the most important feedback does not come through any solicitation; it can only be observed. After this fateful breakfast experience I sat down and made a list of everything I felt I knew about the guests coming to the Mansion. This time my focus was on their behaviors and what those behaviors told me about their wants and needs. My analysis led me to one conclusion: Limit the experience but knock it out of the park on delivery.

Here's an example of how this philosophy played out at the Mansion:

✓ Streamlined offering: Ditch the 5 course breakfast offering a selection of the finest teas, strong coffee with cream, chocolate shavings, and freshly squeezed orange and grapefruit juice. And, of course, a variety of morning newspapers!

✓ It's all about the package: My 6 biggest WMDs (weapons of mass differentiation) were Beyonce, Queen Latifah, Lucy B, Sunflower, Phoenix and Gracie... my cruiser bikes. I would mention the bikes but did not make them a key part of my marketing. Every time, and I mean every time, I provided complimentary use of the bikes the guests came back raving about them. They were cool and Denver is such a bike-friendly city. By not offering use of the bikes as a key component of the stay, I was keeping my best marketing angle held captive in my garage. In retrospect, rather than a B & B I should have marketing the experience as a B, B & B (Bed, Bikes and Beverages).

✓ Price out the experience: No one likes additional fees popping up. Once I knew what my guests wanted from their visit at the Mansion, I needed to set one price for that entire experience. Once again, people loved the bikes once they used them but they wouldn't pay a fee for them when it was an additional charge. Priced as an all-inclusive, guests know exactly what they are paying for and they can just relax and have fun.

WhtWldSusanSay@twitter.com

"Surveys are useless and waste of time... besides, a wrong turn will often bring you to exactly the right place."

What Would You Say?

_____

_____

_____

_____

_____

_____

_____

_____

_____

_____

_____

_____

_____

_____

_____

_____

_____

_____

_____

_____

Six
Mansions have stained glass windows for a reason.

<hr>

Six months into Mansion operation, the Mansion was buzzing! Man, did I have my system dialed in. The online booking platform was providing a steady stream of reservations, social media was pinging away, the loft's third shower had been successfully installed and the Emerson Mansion's first suite with private bath was ready to be unveiled.

My operations manual was proving to be invaluable to my sanity (which is always in question). I could turn over the entire Mansion's eight rooms in less than 3 hours giving me an hour of free-time between check-out and check-in. (Think of the possibilities! Perhaps even time for a quickie!). My scaled-down breakfast and scaled-up cocktail hour changed the dynamics of the Mansion giving me the freedom to engage with my guests in a more relaxed and casual manner. The keyless entry pad on the front door changed my role to be less like a babysitter and more like a proprietor which increased my overall happiness ten-fold. I had ads running at the local college for a live-in student to work the main lobby and be night attendant in exchange of room & board. I was back to networking and scouting for all sources of revenue. I finally felt I had some energy to up my game. And, then, an idea came to me.

The main level of the Mansion had always been set up for

small to medium size meetings. I had a total of 5 meeting room spaces, complete with audio/visual equipment but the only type of meetings I had attracted were the local neighborhood associations or non-profit organizations looking for a cost effective (read: free) meeting space. My thought was to offer the space for the meetings at no charge and have beer and wine available for purchase at a reasonable price. I could easily make up the difference of the meeting space fee in beverage sales. There seemed to be a need so why not make the Emerson Mansion the neighborhood gathering spot?

I contacted the law firm known as the best in town for dealing with liquor licenses. We spoke about what my long term goals were and explored a strategy to operate under the radar temporarily while I determined if the model would generate traction with the community and then proceed to the next step; to get a zoning change in place, then apply for a beer and wine permit. I knew better than to launch ahead; it was necessary to take this one step at a time. It seemed that the key to my success was to become fully acquainted with the infamous Registered Neighborhood Communities, who were notoriously known throughout the city to oppose and obstruct changes of this nature. Naively, I thought I could love them up a bit, explain my idea and how it would build community and they would eventually come around. I couldn't have been more wrong.

While this may be a broad generalization, my experience

of Registered Neighborhood Communities is this: They are the equivalent of competitive sport teams but with exceptionally bad manners and poor sportsmanship; the commonality that they probably share is that as kids perhaps they were bullied on the playground, perhaps they were the last to be picked for activities; perhaps they spent a lot of time either in the corner sulking, picking their noses, or tattling on others. As adults, they join together to form an alliance of mean, vicious, unhappy people.

Unfortunately, in the neighborhood with the Mansion there were 8 different associations from which I received copious calls and visits (both unannounced and announced) all demanding to know about my gig. At first I was taken aback by the insistence. Eventually, I figured "what the heck," I will face this head-on and host a meeting to tell them about me, my vision, and field their questions and concerns. This was THE biggest mistake I would make and one that, ultimately, would be the demise of the Emerson Mansion.

Prior to the big meeting, an entourage, whom I came to affectionately refer to as two grunts and a runt stopped by for an "inspection." Two grunts and the runt were intrusive, bitter, and even had the audacity to ask me where I got my money to own the mansion. Little did I know my visit from two grunts and a runt was just the sweet foreshadowing to the general meeting which was a complete debacle. A yelling match broke out in my conference room, not between me and them but between themselves. Have you heard the phrase "shit show"? This was text-book.

By laying all my cards on the table and providing far too much information, I opened a HUGE can of worms prior to the zoning hearing. Why did I have a house full of angry, aggressive people whom I didn't even know weighing in on this business decision? In an attempt to derail my progress, one of the friendly RNC members called and requested an inspection of the building which kicked off a debilitating expensive code-compliance nightmare.

So What?

Transparency has become such a buzz word lately in business and in marketing. It is easy to get tricked into thinking that when it comes to informing the public, more is better. Not true. More information does not make you look more professional, more credible, or more established. Let me be clear, I am absolutely not advocating deceiving the public in any way but as a business-owner you have the right to choose what information you disperse and how you respond to the information pushed out by others. There is an art, particularly in today's social marketing landscape, to being open and available to the public while still maintaining control over the integrity of your business communication. Too much transparency leads to drama, and if there is one thing you can and should eliminate from your business dealings, it's drama. Drama creates emotional baggage and blurs the lines of decision making.

Although you should be visible to your clients, employees and community, you don't always need to be front and center. Sometimes operating in the shadows is just as empowering, if not more. Make your decisions then strategically release communication around these decisions, procedures and policies. You have a brand to protect, a business to grow, and a product or service to deliver. You do not need to deliver background noise, historical data, or futuristic visions that may or may come to fruition.

Now What?

Not having boundaries can blow up on you. Our society is built on sharing and sensationalism. The internet is an amazing vehicle in which to connect, reconnect and stay connected. The ability to communicate to mass audiences on a 24/7 basis has changed the business owner and consumer expectations but that doesn't mean you blindly jump into that wormhole. Not having boundaries deeply rooted in your business communication plan could have devastating results; in your day to day operations and in the social media arena. Having boundaries does not mean invisible, dishonest, non-communicative but choosing what you share with whom and when and how that sharing is done.

✓ Define your boundaries with customers, competitors, business partners, and community members.

- ✓ Build a matrix and be strategic with that information.
- ✓ Keep your different constituents on a need to know basis.
- ✓ Accountant and attorney will have different levels of information, the next level would be your Advisory board
- ✓ Family members (depending on their involvement in the business) should have information boundaries as well.
- ✓ Each audience will require a different communication method.
- ✓ Strategically determine how these groups want to receive information from you.
- ✓ How much access will you allow the public to have to you?
- ✓ Limit access to you by installing gatekeepers, and become semi-invisible.
- ✓ Allow employees to communicate policies and procedures. This will allow for a buffer to be in place between you and your clients.

WhtWldSusanSay@twitter.com

"Obscurity need not be an obstacle to success."

What Would You Say?

_____

_____

_____

_____

_____

_____

_____

_____

_____

_____

_____

_____

_____

_____

_____

_____

_____

_____

Seven
Losing my panties in the Mansion

The moment the "Open" sign lit up the porch of the Mansion, the first arrivals to my doorstep were not customers. Vendors of all shapes and sizes were practically clawing at the ornate wood door, each offering the key to my success through the use of their services and solutions. Armed with slick marketing gimmicks and well-crafted statistics on the Denver market, each of my solicitors had ideas about my business model and how to drive traffic, foot and digital. I give credit to the many ingenious approaches and would often marvel at their tenacity but I could normally decipher a bullshit pitch a mile away.

There was one idea, however, that I fell for against all my better judgment. The idea was that the Mansion would become a small wedding venue. Undoubtedly, the Mansion had some very unique features which gave it the appearance of being a great location for a small wedding; the winding staircase for the dreamy bridal entrance, elegant photo op spots in nearly every room, guest bedrooms for the immediate family, and magnificent acoustics. Here's the catch - the Mansion could only accommodate a parties of 50 or less. Ideal if you're either totally anti-social or don't mind pissing a lot of people off. Otherwise, it's not very realistic. Even those with the best intentions for intimate nuptials end up pushing over that number. But the proponents of this idea were obsessed with the new buzz word "boutique" and eventually I caught the fever and acquiesced to spending a large chunk of change on advertising specific to the boutique wedding space. I was delusional with the Asian flu. Not only do I have a secret distaste for weddings, the only wedding I have ever planned was mine over 30 years ago when a quick $1,000 was all it took for rental bridal costumes, a few bouquets of carnations, and a honeymoon at the local Holiday Inn. Other than the time I flew 1,000+ miles to have dinner with a guy I'd just met online, this was the craziest thing I had ever gotten myself into.

The potential for revenue looked promising and I had a host of people swearing this was a brilliant plan so I jumped in feet first. I hosted cocktail receptions for wedding planners, florists, bakers, caterers and photographers, hoping to build awareness of the Emerson Mansion as THE Denver boutique wedding venue. I invited (at no cost) photographers to stage wedding photo shoots, complete with flowers, cake, and fake brides and grooms. Sure enough, within a month of advertising I started receiving email and telephone inquiries. The pictures were stunning, the parties fun, but after all the activity and expense, I booked only one wedding. They signed the contract and paid in-full within 24 hours of site visit. Score! Or so I thought. Then, a short time later the bride, the mother of the bride and the bride's sister came for a site visit. The mother had not a kind word to say about the Mansion and was so generally negative about the bride's matrimonial vision that she had her daughter in tears within minutes of the meeting's commencement. On hindsight I should have refunded the money and cancelled the reservation, and perhaps even offered the mother money to go away forever. But I pressed on, overflowing with wedding-planning naiveté.

Just a few months was all the time needed for that wedding to morph into a DIY wedding for over 100 featuring catered food appropriate for a family of five, homemade cupcakes, one keg of Budweiser, several pitchers of ice tea, lemonade, water, and a half dozen tables and chairs with no floral arrangements or decorations. They actually brought in old books wrapped in wilted brown paper from a rummage sale and mismatched plates to stage the area alongside their homemade sprinkled cupcakes. It was like watching a Clampett Hillbilly reality show rehearsal in my own home. Just when I thought it couldn't get worse, the wedding was held at 5 PM on one of the hottest recorded days in Denver history and, although we had cleared out the entire Mansion for setup, relatives started gathering as early as 8 AM making setup next to impossible. Where was I during all of this chaos? Hiding in a closet, sweating my ass off, wishing the nightmare would end.

So What?

My passion just wasn't in pitching weddings at the Mansion. It never felt right. Boutique implies small but elite. So although the mansion was small, what I had to offer was not elite. I needed to be realistic and not be everything to everyone. I oversold myself, the Mansion and my ability to deliver.

My venue was unique, sophisticated, and intimate and oriented to details. I should have played to my strengths and not re-engineer myself into a niche that I could not support, deliver or even desired. However, there was a niche I could have owned and occupied very naturally. The Mansion was a perfect place for bachelor/bachelorette parties, pre-nuptial dinners, and photo sessions. With the proximity of downtown Denver, multiple concert venues, fabulous bars, restaurants, the abundance of great weather and, my most powerful attraction, the cruiser bikes, I could provide a real WOW experience for the events surrounding and leading up to a wedding. But NOT the wedding.

By trying to stage weddings, I was like Cinderella's step sisters, squeezing my feet into the slippers that did not fit at the encouragement of a deranged mother.

Now what?

✓ Don't let people tell you what your business model is. You know what you want out of the business.

✓ Disqualify yourself.

✓ In a world of gurus and experts. It's too easy to be an expert and to misrepresent what you can do. It's a trap, don't do it.

✓ Be wary of opportunists or vendors that are trying to

get you to pitch your business a certain way. What's in it for them?

✓ It is up to you to know your business and your limits. It is the business owner's responsibility to guide the customer into an experience that is going to be exceptional.

✓ You have to know your business better than they do.

✓ Give a shit.

WhtWldSusanSay@twitter.com

"For $28,000, the average cost of a wedding, invest in a justice of the peace, multiple plastic surgeries, and a retainer for a good divorce attorney."

➤ What Would You Say?

_____

_____

_____

_____

_____

_____

_____

_____

_____

_____

_____

_____

_____

_____

_____

_____

_____

_____

_____

_____

Eight
Isolation & Loneliness distorts any situation

Although the zoning meeting with the neighbor organizations turned out to be a total disaster, it was nothing in comparison to what would happen next. As if I hadn't learned my lesson on transparency already, the universe apparently needed to drive that nail in just a little further. As both my phone and email were pinging out of control with interview requests from the neighborhood newsletters, I held tight to my new-found communication strategy rooted in the philosophy that less is more. The zoning hearing was a week away and I was conflicted as to whether to personally attend or send an attorney as my advocate. Either way, I knew the hearing was going to be tumultuous at best. The thought of pulling my zoning request and operating under the radar was becoming more and more appealing. I just needed time; time to sort out all my options.

It was 9:00 am on a Friday and my last guest had departed for the day, and the weekend and upcoming week was booked to capacity. I was just ready to roll out for quick bike ride when I noticed a missed called, so I quickly checked the voice message. To my ultimate surprise, the message was from the Denver Fire Department. It went like this, "Hey Susan, this is the Denver Fire Department. We received a neighborhood complaint that alleges you are operating a Bed & Breakfast at 1601 Emerson. I did notice that you have your B&B permit, but did not change the occupancy use on the building. Please call me. I stopped by earlier but the gate was locked and I would like to schedule an inspection"

I was stunned, unable to move. This could not be happening; I did all of my due diligence prior to closing on the Mansion. My commercial real estate agent never once mentioned anything about a change of occupancy, only the need to obtain a bed & breakfast permit. I immediately placed a call to my real estate agent, who went dead silent on the other end. I didn't call her to engage in the blame game, I was looking for answers and solutions. My next call was to my architect to determine if I was indeed out of compliance and, more importantly, to gather info on the quickest way to rectify the situation. I needed to buy some time to figure out my options. In the end there was no quick, and certainly no inexpensive, option. After scheduling appointments with the building permit department and pleading to both my city Councilman and the Mayor, the news kept getting worse by the day. Over the next couple weeks, I warded off a Cease and Desist order from the Fire Department but, as my cries for help went unanswered, I knew it was only a matter of time before they shut down the B & B.

B & Bs had recently fallen into a new category that required an internal sprinkler system and ADA compliance. For a historic mansion built in 1899 getting sprinkler companies to bid on the project was next to impossible. If I had followed the proper permitting process 6 months earlier I could have been grandfathered in. To make matters worse, I was required to hire an architect, structural engineer, and submit plans that would take a minimum of 3 months to review. I inquired about operating on a temporary permit while I either got a variance or completed the work; the question was met with a chuckle and emphatic head shake. I tallied the costs to a nice round figure of at least $175,000 to get into compliance combined with a loss income of 3 to 4 months, which added another $40,000. I was screwed.

There was one saving grace which bought me a tiny, little bit of time. When the Fire Department came by for their inspection, it happened as the Mansion was in the full throws of a boudoir photo shoot. As scantily clad models strutted about the Mansion in sexy lingerie, the firemen had a hard time (pun intended) staying focused on the task at hand. If I had known then that I would be writing this book, I couldn't have made up a better story. Looking back, the absurdity of the situation was mind-blowingly beautiful.

The arrival of the Cease & Desist order from the Fire Department marked the lowest point in my life. As a very independent woman I have always enjoyed my autonomy but, for the first time in my life, being alone really made a difference. With no business partner, no bedroom partner, my son deployed to a far off country; the only family that mattered was my mother who lived nearby but was very fragile and aging. For all intents and purposes, I was alone. I had accomplished so much by myself but I felt I could no longer go it alone.

I packed up my car and headed to Nebraska to visit my mother in search of refuge and advice. I rarely sought out my mother's advice nor did she often give it. However, after arriving I slept for 3 days straight and when I woke up, she looked into my eyes, and she said, "You make me so proud. I never saw your Mansion, but I know you and your capabilities. Things happen and now you need to get into your car, drive back to Denver, and clean up your mess!" I will never forget those words. Ever.

In that moment, it became clear that I needed to fold my business and mitigate my losses. By being proactive and realistic about what the numbers were telling me about the future of this business, I could back out strategically, knowing that I had given my very best. I hugged my mom for what would be the last time; she passed away several months later. That single hug gave me the courage and strength to go back to Denver and do what I needed to do.

So What?

Creating a balance between your professional and personal life is daunting. The lines are blurry. Malcolm Gladwell in his book *Outliers*, speaks about what separates really successful people from mediocrity; IQ, opportunity, and economic status all play into it but one factor often overlooked is the personal support system. Getting help along the way is critical, "and no-one – not rock stars, not professional athletes, not software billionaires, and not even geniuses – ever make it alone." (Galdwell, 2008)

Whether it's a business partner, a bedroom partner, or a personal confidant, find somebody who understands your personal fears and frustrations and with whom you feel comfortable sharing your personal and business highs and lows. This person is very different from your advisory board; this person is someone who can offer emotional support through the many decisions you will need to make along the way. They have seen you without the "window dressing," they understand your vulnerabilities. They are there for you when you need them. When you are forced to make every decision alone and you have no sounding board, situations get blown out of proportion. This was my reality. In the end, what pushed me to walk away wasn't the zoning problems or the Neighborhood Associations, it wasn't the lack of sleep or the necessity for an operations manual, and it wasn't even lackluster new business opportunities. No, I simply did not want to keep fighting this fight alone.

A note about the professionals you hire: make sure they clearly understand your business model and how your business will be affected by the laws and regulations within their area expertise. Maintain a healthy and professional distance with these professionals; they are not your confidantes. If these professionals are friends, new or longstanding, make sure that in return for their payment or a commission they are committed to representing your best interests at all times. No excuses. You are paying for their expertise, hold them accountable. Also, when paying for a professional's knowledge, follow their advice. If you decide not to heed their advice, fully understand the ramifications. No brainer, right? You'd be surprised how many people pay somebody to give them professional guidance and then proceed to do the opposite.

Now What?

✓ What is the least likely scenario to happen?

✓ Plan for it!

✓ Create a variety of scenarios and contingency plans.

✓ Just like a disaster recovery plans that used in natural disasters what is your disaster recovery plan or exit strategy?

✓ What happens if you get sick or disabled?

✓ Who is your emotional counterweight in your life?

✓ Who can you have pillow talk with?

WhtWldSusanSay@twitter.com

"In life, generally less is more with the sole exception of pillow talk."

What Would You Say?

_____

_____

_____

_____

_____

_____

_____

_____

_____

_____

_____

_____

_____

_____

_____

_____

_____

Nine
Revenge of the Mansion

← ·◉· →

As I drove from Nebraska back to Denver "to clean up my mess," per my mother's instructions, my head ached thinking of how I would land on the right resolution with the Mansion. Should I tackle City Hall, the neighborhood associations, and rebuild my bed & breakfast business? Was there a different business that would emerge as a viable option, allowing me to quickly recoup my losses and move towards positive ROI with the Mansion? Could I, should I, and would I be willing to attempt to operate under the radar? Or... should I just cut my losses and sell the Mansion? Each scenario had its pros and cons. To organize my thoughts, I created a spreadsheet where I separated my emotional and business positions on each option. In the end, the financials of continuing to operate the Mansion outweighed the opportunities. The obvious choice became clear; I needed to lose the Mansion.

Once I listed the Mansion for sale, it was amazing the number vultures that swooped in to see how they could get the Mansion at a rock bottom price.

After several failed contracts, a legitimate buyer finally emerged. Although the Mansion was zoned for either commercial or residential use, it was more likely to stay commercial due to the obvious potential for a commercial buyer and it hadn't been a residence since the early 1930s. Upon going into contract I did not know, nor care, what this particular buyer planned for the Mansion though I assumed it was for commercial purposes. All I cared about was getting to closing; every day the Mansion remained in my name, my bank account hemorrhaged. Miraculously, we closed in warp speed.

I met the buyer for the first time the day of closing. When he walked in with a body guard, I had a sneaking suspicion that the perfect end to this outrageous drama was soon to be revealed. He was not from Colorado, he was from back East. He immediately opened the conversation by alerting me that he had done some background research on me and knew of my illicit business with the Mansion. It turns out his "intelligence" came from a cursory online stalking mission and quizzing the many neighborhood watchdogs. He was thrilled to report that the neighborhood was ecstatic about the new ownership in hopes of seeing the Mansion turned back into a residence. Then, with a sadistic chuckle, he says, "If they were upset about you and what you were doing with the Mansion, they are really going to hate me!" This had all the earmarks of being too good to be true. My suspicions were dead on; it was the perfect ending.

The new owner had been searching for a residence in Denver, the up and coming Marijuana Capital of the United States, with a basement large enough to allow him to install a full-scale marijuana growing operation. With the flexibility of converting the Mansion to residential use, that would release him from certain restrictions that would otherwise force him to adhere and be under scrutiny of the city. His plans entailed to host 4:20 parties (4:20 being slang term that refers to smoking marijuana) every afternoon on the main floor of the Mansion. As a self described pot aficionado, he had every intention of making the most of the new lenient laws around his favorite plant.

It has been over 6 months, and recently I drove by the Mansion. It looks empty and vacant. The grounds which once were vibrant green and lush are now weedy and brown and un-kept. I know he's moved ahead with his plans because a few of his 4:20 party patrons have mistakenly posted about their love of his product on the Emerson Mansion Facebook page which I own and retain the rights to. As far as the neighborhood's knowledge and feelings around the 4:20 parties and how they're getting along with their new neighbor, I can only imagine and when I do, I find that a smile spreads across my face. I bet, right about now, my wine parties are looking pretty fucking tame. Revenge is so sweet.

So What?

There is an old Buddha saying, "Everything eventually falls apart," with no exceptions. The things that surround will all disappear: furniture, homes, buildings, relationships, our bodies, our minds, cities, institutions, and perhaps eventually our planet. It may take weeks, months, years, decades or centuries but eventually everything... and I mean everything falls apart. What we can control is how we learn and grow from the "things" before they fall apart; what we feed our minds and bodies, how we nurture our friendships, family and lovers. How do we care for our homes, how do we interact with businesses and institutions, do we pick up our trash and are we mindful of minimizing our footprint by not wasting our natural resources while we are on Mother Earth? When things begin to fall apart, recognize it early, minimize the damage, and always remember the life lessons found within the experience.

It makes me think of the Kenny Rogers's song, The Gambler, "The secret to surviving is to know when to hold em and know when to fold em... Know when to walk away, and know when to run... know when you are out of aces ... and there will be a time enough to count them when the dealing's done." (Rogers)

Limit your time traveling. By "time traveling" I mean time which is spent either reminiscing about the past or worrying about the future. (Aulcher) Try to concentrate on THIS moment. We all are guilty of inordinate amounts of time travel, each of us to different extents. However, realize things are falling apart around us every day and there is nothing you can do about it. There is peace within accepting that fact.

Limit long-reach projections. 3 - 6 year business plans are unproductive. They stop you from making a decision right now in this moment. Banks and lenders want predictive models. They are useless bullshit. Plan constantly for reinvention. Expect that your role, your business, your life will change dramatically sometime soon. Because it will. It is the nature of the extremely non-static world we live in.

Now What?

Of the 6 million small businesses out there, most owners or proprietors aren't in business to build something big. They aren't trying to build the next Internet wonder, or create the next world-changing gadget or gizmo. Most small business people are in it for one reason: FREEDOM!

Three out of four entrepreneurs get up each morning with the simple yearning for total, complete, unimpeded independence. They must be their own boss or they can't cope with the day. They cannot be employed at IBM or even at a local car dealership because they are like the coyote -- they can never be domesticated. Are you among them?

✓ Do you have disaster recovery plan?

✓ What types of crises could develop?

✓ What is your exit strategy?

✓ How will you know to when to implement it?

WhtWldSusanSay@twitter.com

"Be aware of your surroundings; notice the impact that your words and actions have on others. For every action there is a reaction. Take care of yourself. Read, write, listen to music, and wear really cute shoes. Being practical is so over-rated".

What Would You Say?

Resources

Altucher, J. (2013). Choose Yourself Be Happy, Make Millions, Live the Dream. *Lioncrest. (pg 50, 184)*

Clifton, D. /Buckingham, M. (2001). Now, Discover Your Strengths. *New York City: The Free Press; A Division of Simon & Schuster Inc.*

Galdwell, M. (2008). Outliers. *New York: Back Bay Books/Little, Brown and Company. (page 115)*

Gerber, M. E. (1995). The E Myth Revisited. *New York City: HarperCollins. (pgs 197-217)*

T. (2007). Strengths Finder 2.0. New York City: *Gallup Press.*

Rogers, K. (1978 Composer). The Gambler. *Capitol Records*

Sinek, S. (2009). Start With Why. *New York City: Penguin Group. (pages 56, 57, 184)*

Special Contributions

Greg Grey for "What, So What and Now What" book format.
Jay Hanna for Restoring Sanity back into my Life, and by agreeing to be my CPA.
Teresa Porter for "Can't Fix Stupid".

About the Author – Susan Underhill

Susan is currently serving as President for fit, fueled & focused, Inc., a business offering total rejuvenation for females in need of an escape from the demands of balancing careers with a busy personal life. Through 25+ years in senior leadership positions at a Fortune 50 company, Susan became passionate about creating a business that would fulfill this need through an intensive focus on fitness, healthy diet, and inspirational outlets.

In pursuit of this vision in July 2011, Susan purchased and renovated a historic Mansion in downtown Denver, Colorado. Due to the unique charm and downtown location, the Mansion became a bed/breakfast destination that offered a healthy niche in the convention/tourism industry as a boutique B&B. During this short tenure, she was able to achieve outstanding results in developing online marketing tactics that drove top rankings in Internet searches, and reviews. Over 450 clients from 20 different countries each with an unique and endearing story experience the Emerson Mansion. In April of 2013, she sold the Mansion to refocus her energies in developing marketing, sales, and management solutions in lieu of operating the Emerson Mansion.

Ms. Underhill received her M.B.A. from Thunderbird School of Global Management and her undergraduate degree in Political Science & Psychology from University of Nebraska. She has one son, Zachary who is serving in the US military. Susan's infectious laugh fills a room and her intellect, eclectic mix of experiences, and never-ending wit makes her the perfect wine-drinking buddy.

Please connect with her...
Web Site: fitfueledfocused.com or
Email: susan@fitfueledfocused.com

By Susan Underhill

Cindy Cragg - Copy Editor, Expurgator, and Project Manager
ex·pur·gate, ex·pur·gat·ed, ex·pur·gat·ing, ex·pur·gates
To remove erroneous, vulgar, obscene, or otherwise objectionable
material from a book before publication.

Dawn Bowman - Illustrator, Imagery Consultant, and Mystic
mys·tic, mys·ti·cal, mys·ti·cism, mys·ti·cal·ness
Someone who transforms visions into reality.

9 780692 772348